boyzone | a diffe

D1589071

Wise Publications

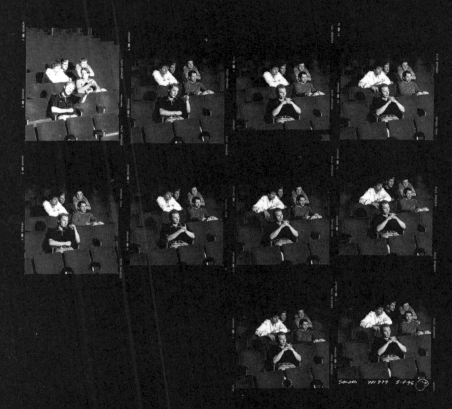

This publication is not authorised
for sale in the United States of America
and/or Canada

250 340 743

Wise Publications
London / New York / Sydney / Paris / Copenhagen / Madrid

KIRKLEES CULTURAL
SERVICES

ACC. NO. 250 340 743

CLASS 780

DEPT DE CHECKED

MF	RAV	DMR
DE 1/98	CH	TH

Exclusive Distributors:
Music Sales Limited
8/9 Frith Street,
London W1V 5TZ, England.
Music Sales Pty Limited
120 Rothschild Avenue
Rosebery, NSW 2018, Australia.

Order No.AM941644
ISBN 0-7119-6230-8
This book © Copyright 1996 by Wise Publications.
Visit the Internet Music Shop at
http://www.musicsales.co.uk

Unauthorised reproduction of any part of this
publication by any means including photocopying is
an infringement of copyright.

Music arranged by Roger Day.
Music processed by Paul Ewers Music Design.

Printed in the United Kingdom by
Page Brothers ltd, Norwich, Norfolk.

Your Guarantee of Quality:
As publishers, we strive to produce every book to
the highest commercial standards.
The music has been freshly engraved and, whilst
endeavouring to retain the original running order of
the recorded album, the book has been carefully
designed to minimise awkward page turns and to
make playing from it a real pleasure.
Particular care has been given to specifying acid-free,
neutral-sized paper made from pulps which have
not been elemental chlorine bleached.
This pulp is from farmed sustainable forests and was
produced with special regard for the environment.
Throughout, the printing and binding have been
planned to ensure a sturdy, attractive publication
which should give years of enjoyment. If your copy
fails to meet our high standards, please inform us
and we will gladly replace it.

Music Sales' complete catalogue describes thousands
of titles and is available in full colour sections by subject,
direct from Music Sales Limited.
Please state your areas of interest and send a cheque/postal
order for £1.50 for postage to: Music Sales Limited,
Newmarket Road, Bury St. Edmunds, Suffolk IP33 3YB.

9. **Paradise**

14. **A Different Beat**

22. **Melting Pot**

19. **Ben**

28. **Don't Stop Looking For Love**

33. **Isn't It A Wonder**

38. **Words**

42. **It's Time**

48. **Games Of Love**

52. **Strong Enough**

56. **Heaven Knows**

62. **Crying In The Night**

65. **Give A Little**

70. **She Moves Through The Fair**

It's not often that you find someone
Who can fulfil all your dreams inside
It's like an angel from above
She was the one for me, believe

But it doesn't wither like a flower in snow
I always wanted you to know

We're going to build a bridge,
between our hearts
Going to cross the river of love
Into paradise, paradise
Going to walk up the road, hand in hand
To the castle in the sky
Where we're gonna live
Gonna live, yeah

And when she opens up her eyes
It's like a perfect sunrise outside
I put my fingers through her hair
And it feels like silk to me

But it doesn't wither like a flower in snow
I always wanted to know

We're going to build a bridge,
between our hearts
Going to cross the river of love
Into paradise, paradise
Going to walk up the road, hand in hand
To the castle in the sky
Where we're gonna live
Gonna live, yeah

Yeah Yeah Yeah Yeah

Don't you know
We're going to build a
bridge between our hearts
Going to cross the river of love
Into paradise, paradise

We're going to build a bridge,
between our hearts
Going to cross the river of love
Into paradise, paradise
Going to walk up the road, hand in hand
To the castle in the sky
Where we're gonna live
Gonna live, yeah

Let's not forget this place
Let's not neglect our race
Let unity become
Life on earth be one

So let me take your hand
We are but grains of sand
Born through the winds of time
Given a special sign

So let's take a stand
And look around us now, people
So let's take a stand
And look around us now, people

Eeyea - oh, Eeyea - oh, by - yah
To a different beat
Eeyea - oh, Eeyea - Eeyca - oh, by - yah

Humanity has lost face
Let's understand its grace
Each day at a time
Each life including mine

So let's take a stand
And look around us now, people
So let's take a stand
And look around us now, people
Oh people, oh people

Eeyea - oh, Eeyea - oh, by - yah
To a different beat
Eeyea - oh, Eeyea - Eeyca - oh, by - yah

I've seen the rain fall in Africa
I've touched the snows of Alaska
(oh tell me now)
I've felt the mists of Niagara
Now I believe in you

Eeyea - oh, Eeyea - oh, by - yah
To a different beat
Eeyea - oh, Eeyea - Eeyca - oh, by - yah

Eeyea - oh, Eeyea - oh, by - yah
To a different beat
Eeyea - oh, Eeyea - Eeyca - oh, by - yah

How far we've come and how far to go
Rain does not fall on one roof alone

Take a pinch of one man
Wrap him up in suntan
Add a touch of blue-blood
And a little bitty bit of
whatever you choose

Curly black and blond
Mix it with love and let's see
If you lump it altogether
Well you've got a recipe
for a get along scene...
Oh what a beautiful dream
If it could only come true
you know you know

What we need is a great big melting pot
Big enough to take the world
And all it's got
Keep it stirring for a hundred
years or more
Turn out coffee coloured
people by the score
Yeah... no

Mick and Lady Faithful
And everyone who's graceful
You know the living could be tasteful
As we should all get together
in a mixing machine
Yeah Yeah Yeah

The poorest and the wealthy
Weakest and the healthy
If you lump us all together
Well you gotta recipe
for a get along scene
I'd better call up the Queen
It's only fair that she know
you know you know

, the two of us need look no more
 both found what we're looking for
 a friend to call my own
 never be alone
 you, my friend, will see
 got a friend in me

, you're always running here and there
 feel you're not wanted anywhere
 ou ever look behind
 don't like what you find
 re's one thing you should know
 got a place to go

ed to say "I" and "Me"
 it's "Us", Now it's "We"
ed to say "I" and "Me"
 it's "Us", Now it's "We"

, most people would turn you away
, the two of us need look no more

n't listen to a word they say
y don't see you as I do
sh they would try to
sure they'd think again
ey had a friend like Ben.

Been so long since I found someone
You came as some surprise
But I knew you were meant for me
When I looked into your eyes
So beautiful and strong
Boy where did you come from
As life passed me by
You fell from the sky and
I could hear you say

Don't stop looking for love
It can be found in the strangest places
Just when you've given up
Along comes a miracle that turns
your life around
So don't stop looking for love

Walking around with my head hanging
down I felt so all alone
And your love seemed miles away
I was a heart without a home
A woman in the rain you took the clouds away
Now bright as the sun, our love has begun
And I could hear you say

Don't stop looking for love
It can be found in the strangest places
Just when you've given up
Along comes a miracle that turns
your life around
So don't stop looking for love

Suddenly my dream had
come and rescued me
I can't believe I finally reached the day
Now I can say

Don't stop looking for love
It can be found in the strangest places
Just when you've given up
Along comes a miracle that turns
your life around
So don't stop looking for love

It's a sign of the times girl,
sad songs on the radio
It's a sign of the times girl,
as the leaves begin to go
But all these signs now,
showing on my face
Proving me wrong, taking its place

And I pray to God
That there's more that we can do, yeah
And I pray to God
That there's more that we can show
More that we can do, yeah

Isn't it a wonder, as a new
-born bay cries
And isn't it a wonder, with
the sweetness in my eyes
And isn't it a wonder, at the
crossroads of my life
Isn't it a wonder?
Isn't it a wonder, to me?

It's the way of the world when,
wrong takes hold of right
It's the way of the world, in which
we've all lost sight
But isn't this world too simple to be true
Holding on to memories of you

And I pray to God
That there's more that we can do, yeah
And I pray to God
That there's more that we can show
More than we can do, yeah

Isn't it a wonder, as a new
-born bay cries
And isn't it a wonder, with
the sweetness in my eyes
And isn't it a wonder, at the
crossroads of my life
Isn't it a wonder?
Isn't it a wonder, to me?

That I can see a change in me
But I won't go back cause
that's behind me
And after all strong words are spoken
My heart will never be, never be
Never be, never be... broken

Isn't it a wonder, as a new
-born bay cries
And isn't it a wonder, with
the sweetness in my eyes
And isn't it a wonder, at the
crossroads of my life
Isn't it a wonder?
Isn't it a wonder, to me?

Smile an ever lasting smile
A smile can bring you near to me
Don't ever let me find you gone
Cause that would bring a tear to me
This world has lost its glory
Let's start a brand new story
Now my love
You think that I don't even mean
A single word I say...

It's only words
And words are all I have
To take your heart away

Talk in ever lasting words and
Dedicate them all to me
And I will give you all my life
I'm here if you should call to me
You think that I don't even mean
a single word I say

It's only words
And words are all I have
To take your heart away

It's only words
And words are all I have
To take your heart away

Da Da Da Da Da Da Da Da
Da Da Da Da Da Da Da Da
Da Da Da Da Da Da Da Da

This world has lost its glory
Let's start a brand new story
Now my love
You think that I don't even mean
A single word I say

It's only words
And words are all I have
To take your heart away

It's only words
And words are all I have
To take your heart away

Here at home, the thoughts
Racing through my crazy mind
Trying to figure out
If I'm loving you this one more time

And when I got the mail
It made me close the door
Just right behind
On a trail of clothes
Left lying here
Thrown across the floor now

Maybe it's the way this love was
Meant to be
And maybe it's the only way for you and me

It's time, to say goodbye
It's time, oh please don't cry girl
It's time, two reasons why
It's time, I will never lie to you

You cast your spell, but the magic
Has been broken down
And I'm all packed up, with empty
Boxes lying all around
It's like a flickering flame, that casts
A shadow on the brightest day
And does it help to know
That I feel the same
And it's gone now

Maybe it's the way this love was
Meant to be
And maybe it's the only way for you and me

It's time, to say goodbye
It's time, oh please don't cry girl
It's time, two reasons why
It's time, I will never lie to you

Many years ago now
In the Garden of Love
A temptation that was watched from above
I'll be your Adam, if you'll be my Eve
So come show me that you will not deceive

That love, just a crazy feeling
Deep and hidden meaning, it's true
And love, takes some understanding
So don't you go and break all the rules

We're talking A-B-C
I'm singing do-re-mi
I'll teach you endlessly
Games of Love

We're counting 1-2-3
I'm writing "U 4 Me"
I'll teach you endlessly
Games of Love

Listen to me now girl
'Cos you've known all along
It's a game of love so don't play it wrong
I'll be your Romeo and you Juliet
Just read the book and you won't forget

That love, just a crazy feeling
Deep and hidden meaning, it's true
And love, takes some understanding
So don't you go and break all the rules

We're talking A-B-C
I'm singing do-re-mi
I'll teach you endlessly
Games of Love

lieve in all that love can bring
n see it's meant to be
we'll be

gether)
e the best in me
ever)
were meant to be
use I know it
I know there's always
come home to
ve is strong enough)

e see us through
ause of you
ow we're strong enough
e see us through
ugh and through
s love's strong enough 4 2

a child I want this love to grow
ny smile I tell it all
we'll be

Tears run dry on a young man's face
Feel the glow of a warm embrace
Been on a boat to the
edge of somewhere
Searched for you almost everywhere
No more hills left for me to bear
Cause now I'm almost there

But baby love's growing much stronger
From the day that you said
you were gonna be mine
From the way I was lead into your mind

Everything comes to those who wait
Like a winter for spring
And the beauty it brings
And everyone searches
For the perfect one
As Heaven Knows
As Heaven Knows

If you believe, like you know that I do
You will see I'm the one for you
Never forget when I take your hand
At last, I'm here, can't you understand
So bring on the night and I'll make it right
Bring a dull day and I'll make it bright
Cause now we're almost there

But baby love's growing much stronger
From the day that you said you were
gonna be mine
From the day I was lead into your mind
Maybe love's making me stronger
From the day that you said you were
gonna be mine
From the way I was lead into your mind

Everything comes to those who wait
Like a winter for spring
And the beauty it brings
And everyone searches
For the perfect one
As Heaven Knows
As Heaven Knows

Alone just sitting here
Thinking of you 'til it hurts
You're young so innocent
Without a care in the world
You're there, but not visible
My expectations become

But do you think it's right?
And do you think it's right?
Crying in the night
For crying in the night
(ooh in the night)

My road was different
There's so much that you have to learn
A little hand in mine
And all the smiles and laughter is fine
Wherever I'll be, land or sea
I will care for thee

But do you think it's right?
And do you think it's right?
Crying in the night
For crying in the night
(ooh in the night)

Each day provides its own gifts
Time brings all to pass
Writing comes more easily
When you've got something to say

You're young and beautiful
Have no enemy but time
In time, take time
When time does last
For time is no time
When time is passed

But do you think it's right?
And do you think it's right?
Crying in the night
For crying in the night
(ooh in the night)

Give a little, take a little, pray a little
Give a little, you know you've got to
Take a little, just one more time
Pray a little, to make it happen

And I'd swear, I'd cross the road
But you'd avoid me
Please tell me, why?
It ain't fair, I'd call you up
But you won't answer
Just no reply

Too blind to see that ache inside
So have a heart I'm begging you

Give a little, take a little, pray a little
Say you want to
Give a little, you know you've got to
Take a little, just one more time
Pray a little, to make it happen
Say you want me, girl

Somehow with every chance
I'll make you happy
You won't believe
Sing out loud with each and every
Waking moment
You'll fill my need

Too blind to see that ache inside
So have a heart, I'm begging you

Give a little, take a little, pray a little
Say you want to
Give a little, you know you've got to
Take a little, just one more time
Pray a little, to make it happen
Say you want me, girl

Say you want me, girl
And wait and see
Too blind to see that ache inside
So have a heart, I'm begging you

Say you want me

Give a little, take a little, pray a little
Say you want to
Give a little, you know you've got to
Take a little, just one more time
Pray a little, to make it happen
Say you want me, girl

My young love said to me
My mother won't mind
And my father won't slight you
For your lack of kind
Then she stepped away from me
And this she did say
"It will not be long love,
till our Wedding day".

She stepped away from me
And she moved through the fair
And fondly I watched her
Moved here and move there
Then she made her way homeward
with one star awake
As the swan in the evening
moves over the lake

I dreamt it last night
That my dead love came in
So softly she moved
That her feet made no din
Then she came close beside me
And this she did say
"It will not be long love
Till our wedding day".

Paradise

boyzone

Words & Music by Martin Brannigan, Ronan Keating & Roy Hedges

© Copyright 1996 PolyGram Music Publishing Limited, 47 British Grove, London W4 (33.33%),
Island Music Limited, 47 British Grove, London W4 (33.33%) & 19 Music/
BMG Music Publishing Limited, 69-79 Fulham High Street, London SW6 (33.34%).
All Rights Reserved. International Copyright Secured.

one for me,— be - lieve.—— But it does-n't with-er like a flow - er in snow,-

I al-ways want-ed you to know,— we're going to

build a bridge— be - tween our hearts,— going to cross the riv - er of love— in-to

pa - ra - dise,— pa - ra - dise, going to walk up that road,—

10

Don't you know we're going to

build a bridge___ be - tween our hearts,___ going to cross the

riv - er of love___ in - to pa - ra - dise,___ pa - ra - dise. Going to

build a bridge___ be - tween our hearts,___ going to cross the

Verse 2:
And when she opens up her eyes
It's like a perfect sunrise outside.
I put my fingers through her hair
And it feels like silk to me.

A Different Beat

Words & Music by Martin Brannigan, Stephen Gately, Ronan Keating,
Shane Lynch, Keith Duffy & Roy Hedges

Let's not for-get this place,— let's not ne-

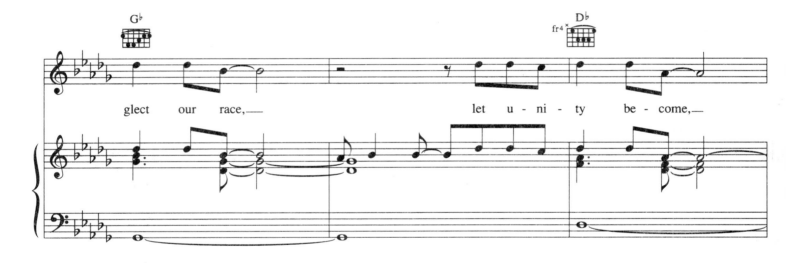

glect our race,— let u-ni-ty be-come,—

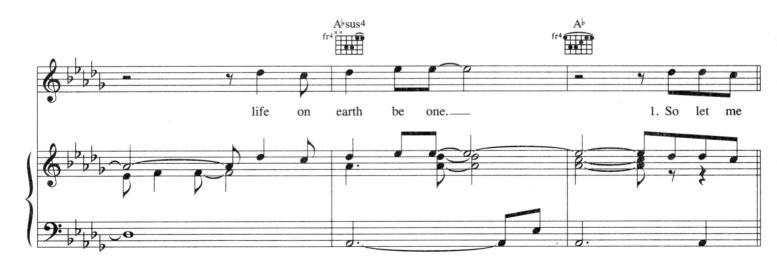

life on earth be one.— 1. So let me

© Copyright 1996 PolyGram Music Publishing Limited, 47 British Grove, London W4 (20%),
Island Music Limited, 47 British Grove, London W4 (60%) & 19 Music/
BMG Music Publishing Limited, 69-79 Fulham High Street, London SW6 (20%).
All Rights Reserved. International Copyright Secured.

yea oh,— ee- yea oh,— ee- yea oh,— by- yah..

(To a dif - fer- ent beat.) Ee - yea oh,— ee- yea oh,— ee-

1. yea oh,— by- yah.— 2. Hu- man- i- **2.**

I've seen the rain fall in Af - ri - ca,— I've touched the snows of A -

16

Verse 2:
Humanity has lost face,
Let's understand its grace,
Each day, one at a time,
Each life, including mine.

Let's take a stand and look around us now,
People,
So let's take a stand and look around us now,
People, oh people, oh people.

Ben | boyzone

Words by Don Black. Music by Walter Scharf

1. Ben, the two of us need look no more, we both found what we were
(Verses 2 & 3 see block lyric)

look-ing for. With a friend to call my own, I'll nev - er be a -

© Copyright 1971, 1972 Jobete Music Company Incorporated, USA.
Jobete Music (UK) Limited, London WC2 for the UK and Eire.
All Rights Reserved. International Copyright Secured.

⊕ *Coda*

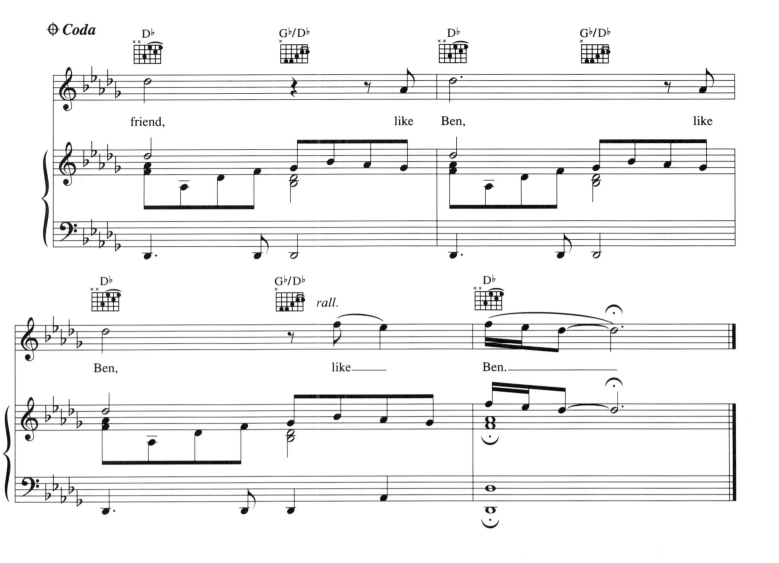

friend,   like Ben,   like

Ben,   like   Ben.

Verse 2:
Ben, you're always running here and there,
You feel you're not wanted anywhere.
If you ever look behind
And don't like what you find,
There's one thing you should know:
You've got a place to go.

Verse 3:
Ben, most people would turn you away,
I don't listen to a word they say.
They don't see you as I do,
I wish they would try to;
I'm sure they'd think again
If they had a friend like Ben.

Melting Pot

Words & Music by Roger Cook & Roger Greenaway

© Copyright 1970 for the World Cookaway Music Limited/
Dick James Music Limited, 47 British Grove, London W4.
All Rights Reserved. International Copyright Secured.

1. Take a pinch of white man,_____
(Verse 2 see block lyric)

wrap it up in black skin,_____

add a touch of blue blood,_____ and a lit-tle bit-ty bit of Red In-

-di-an boy._____

Cur - ly black and kink - y,_____ o - ri - en - tal sex - y,_____ if you lump it all to-geth - er,_____ well you've got a re - ci - pe for a get a-long scene,__ oh what a beau-ti-ful dream,__ if it could on - ly come true, you know,__you know.

What we need___ is___ a great___ big melt - ing pot,___

big e - nough___ to take___ the world___ and all it's got,___ keep it

stir - ring for a hun - dred years___ or_____ more, turn - ing out

cof - fee co - loured peo - ple___ by___ the score.___

1.

Repeat ad lib. to fade

Verse 2:
Rabbis and the friars,
Bishops and the gurus,
We had the Beatles and the sun gods a long time ago (it's true),
But then it really didn't matter what religion you choose.

Mick and Lady Faithful,
Lord and Mrs. Graceful,
You know the living could be tasteful,
Why don't we all get together in a loving machine,
I'd better call up the Queen,
It's only fair that she knows, you know.

Don't Stop Looking For Love

Words & Music by Billy Mann & Brett Laurence

1. Been so long_____ since I found_____ some-one, you
(Verse 2 see block lyric)

came as some_____ sur - prise,_____ but I knew_____

© Copyright 1996 Remann Music/Connotation Music,
administered by Warner Tamerlane Publishing Corporation, USA.
Warner Chappell Music Limited, 129 Park Street, London W1.
All Rights Reserved. International Copyright Secured.

Verse 2:
Walking around with my head hanging down,
I felt so all alone.
And your love seemed miles away,
I was a heart without a home.
A woman in the rain,
You took the clouds away.
Now bright as the sun, our love has begun
And I could hear you say.

Isn't It A Wonder

boyzone

Words & Music by Martin Brannigan, Ronan Keating & Roy Hedges

1. It's a sign of the times girl, sad songs on the ra-di-o.
(Verse 2 see block lyric)

It's a sign of the times girl, as the leaves be-gin to go. But all these signs now,

© Copyright 1996 PolyGram Music Publishing Limited, 47 British Grove, London W4 (33.33%),
Island Music Limited, 47 British Grove, London W4 (33.33%) & 19 Music/
BMG Music Publishing Limited, 69-79 Fulham High Street, London SW6 (33.34%).
All Rights Reserved. International Copyright Secured.

Verse 2:
It's the way of the world
When wrong takes hold of right.
It's the way of the world
In which we've all lost sight.
But isn't this world too simple to be true,
Holding on to memories of you.

boyzone | Words

Words & Music by Barry Gibb, Robin Gibb & Maurice Gibb

1. Smile an ev-er-last-ing smile, a smile can bring you near to me.
(Verses 2 & 3 see block lyric)

© Copyright 1967 & 1975 Gibb Brothers Music.
All Rights Reserved. International Copyright Secured.

It's on-ly words, and words are all I have to take your heart a-

way.

It's on-ly words, and words are all I have to take your heart a-

To Coda ⊕

D.%. al Coda

way.

⊕ *Coda*

It's on - ly words, and words are all I have to take your heart a - way.

Verse 2:
Talk in everlasting words
And dedicate them all to me,
And I will give you all my life,
I'm here if you should call to me.

You think that I don't even mean
A single word I say.

Verse 3:
Da da da da... *etc. (8 bars)*

This world has lost its glory,
Let's start a brand new story now, my love.
You think that I don't even mean
A single word I say.

boyzone | It's Time

Words & Music by Martin Brannigan, Stephen Gately, Ronan Keating,
Shane Lynch, Keith Duffy & Roy Hedges

1. Here at home—
(Verse 2 see block lyric)
the thoughts rac - ing through— my cra -

© Copyright 1996 PolyGram Music Publishing Limited, 47 British Grove, London W4 (17.5%),
Island Music Limited, 47 British Grove, London W4 (66%) & 19 Music/
BMG Music Publishing Limited, 69-79 Fulham High Street, London SW6 (16.5%).
All Rights Reserved. International Copyright Secured.

Verse 2:
You cast your spell,
But the magic has been broken down
And I'm all packed up
With empty boxes lying all around.
It's like a flickering flame
That casts a shadow on the brightest day,
And does it help to know that I feel the same
And it's gone now.

Games Of Love

Words & Music by Martin Brannigan, Stephen Gately & Roy Hedges

1. Ma - ny years a - go now in the gar - den of love, a temp - ta -
(Verse 2 see block lyric)

© Copyright 1996 PolyGram Music Publishing Limited, 47 British Grove, London W4 (33.33%).
Island Music Limited, 47 British Grove, London W4 (33.33%) & 19 Music/
BMG Music Publishing Limited, 69-79 Fulham High Street, London SW6 (33.34%).
All Rights Reserved. International Copyright Secured.

CHORUS

don't you go and break all the rules.___ We're talk-in'

A. B. C.,___ I'm sing-ing do re mi,___ I'll teach you end-less-ly___ games of love.__

We're count-ing 1 2__ 3,___ I'm writ-ing "U 4__ me",__ I'll teach you

end - less - ly,___ games of love___

2º (We're talk - ing

50

Verse 2:
Listen to me now girl 'cause you've known all along
It's a game of love, so don't play it wrong.
I'll be your Romeo and you Juliet
So just read the book and you won't forget.

Strong Enough

Words & Music by Phil Harding, Ian Curnow, Julian Gallagher & Ronan Keating

© Copyright 1996 Island Music Limited, 47 British Grove, London W4 (25%), 19 Music/
BMG Music Publishing Limited, 69-79 Fulham High Street, London SW6 (50%) & Copyright Control (25%).
All Rights Reserved. International Copyright Secured.

e - nough. Love see us through, through and through,

this love is strong e - nough for two. 1. I be - lieve
(Verse 2 see block lyric)

in all that love can bring,

I can see it's meant to be.

Verse 2:
Like a child
I want this love to grow.
In my smile
I tell it all.
So we'll be…

Heaven Knows

Words & Music by Martin Brannigan, Ronan Keating & Roy Hedges

© Copyright 1996 PolyGram Music Publishing Limited, 47 British Grove, London W4 (33.33%),
Island Music Limited, 47 British Grove, London W4 (33.33%) & 19 Music/
BMG Music Publishing Limited, 69-79 Fulham High Street, London SW6 (33.34%).
All Rights Reserved. International Copyright Secured.

56

1. Tears run dry on a young man's face, feel the glow— of a warm em-brace.
(Verse 2 see block lyric)

Been on a boat to the edge of some-where, searched for you— al-most ev-'ry-where.

One more hill babe, and I'll be there, no more pain left for me to bear.— 'Cause

now I'm al-most there.—

2. If

D.%. al Coda

⊕ **Coda**

as hea - ven___ knows,___ as

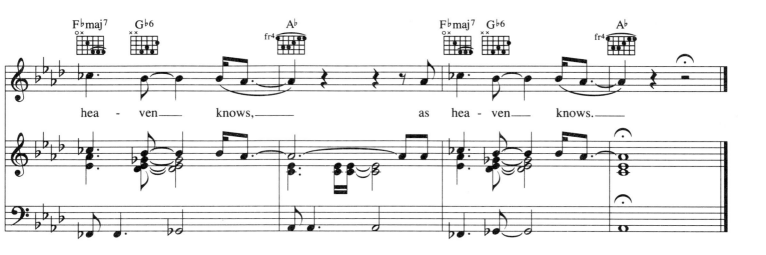

hea - ven___ knows,___ as hea - ven___ knows.___

Verse 2:
If you believe like you know that I do,
You will see I'm the one for you.
Never forget when I take your hand
At last I'm here, can't you understand.
So bring on the night and we'll make it right,
Take a dull day and I'll make it bright.
'Cause now, we're almost there.

Crying In The Night

Words & Music by Martin Brannigan, Stephen Gately, Ronan Keating,
Shane Lynch & Roy Hedges

© Copyright 1996 PolyGram Music Publishing Limited, 47 British Grove, London W4 (28%),
Island Music Limited, 47 British Grove, London W4 (44%) & 19 Music/
BMG Music Publishing Limited, 69-79 Fulham High Street, London SW6 (28%).
All Rights Reserved. International Copyright Secured.

Verse 2:
My road was different,
There's so much that you have to learn.
A little hand in mine,
And all the smiles and laughter is fine.
Wherever I'll be, land or sea,
I will care for thee.

Verse 3:
You're young, you're beautiful,
Have no enemy but time.
And in time, those who take time,
When time does last.
For time is no time
When time is passed.

Give A Little

Words & Music by Martin Brannigan, Stephen Gately & Roy Hedges

© Copyright 1996 PolyGram Music Publishing Limited, 47 British Grove, London W4 (33.33%),
Island Brannic Limited, 47 British Grove, London W4 (33.33%) & 19 Music/
BMG Music Publishing Limited, 69-79 Fulham High Street, London SW6 (33.34%).
All Rights Reserved. International Copyright Secured.

give a lit-tle,   take— a lit-tle,
(You know you've got to.)   (Just one more time.)

pray a lit - tle.

(To make it happen.)

1. And I'd   swear,   I'd cross the road but you'd a - void me,___ please   tell   me   why?
(Verse 2 see block lyric)

___   It ain't   fair,   I'd call you up but you won't ans - wer,___

blind _____ to see ' ___ that ache ___ in - side, ___

so have a heart, I'm beg-ging you. ___

Verse 2:
Somehow with every chance
I'll make you happy,
You won't believe.
Sing out loud
With each and every waking moment,
You'll fill my need.

Traditional. Arranged by Phil Coulter

© Copyright 1996 Four Seasons Music Limited.
All Rights Reserved. International Copyright Secured.

from me___ and this she did___ say, "It___ will not be long love till our wed-ding day."

To Coda ⊕ **1.**

2.

2. She___ lake.

Verse 2:
She stepped away from me,
And she moved through the fair,
And fondly I watched her
Move here and move there.
Then she made her way homeward
With one star awake.
As the swan in the evening
Moves over the lake.

Verse 3:
I dreamt it last night
That my dead love came in,
So softly she moved
That her feet made no din.
Then she came close beside me,
And this she did say,
"It will not be long love
Till our wedding day."